Vegetarian Pressure Cooker

Top 50 Original Vegetarian Meals Ready In Minutes

Make Meat-less, Frugal, And Easy Meals To Use At Home

By: Donna Treston

Table Of Contents

Introduction

Contrary to the beliefs of many, the vegetarian diet is not boring. In fact, it is one of the healthiest ways of eating. The vegetarian diet can provide the body almost all of the essential vitamins and minerals. Plant-based foods are friendly to digestion too and they ensure better nutrient absorption.

The challenge in the vegetarian diet is in the preparation of foods. Lack of cooking skills can lead a vegetarian enthusiast to eat the same foods over and over again. Lack of time can also prevent a vegetarian person from concocting appetizing foods.

Preparing vegetarian foods need not be stressful. It just needs a little bit of creativity and effective technique. That is why this book is created for those who want to make sumptuous vegetarian meals the easy way.

Pressure cooking is the most convenient way to cook delicious and balanced vegan meals. All ingredients can be thrown in just one pot and can be cooked in just a few minutes.

This book contains top fifty vegetarian meals that can be prepared quickly with the help of the pressure cooker. The tasty and healthy meals are perfect for breakfast, lunch and dinner.

The featured recipes in this book are easy to follow. They only call for ingredients that can be easily found in the nearest supermarket and grocery. They will surely inspire everyone, vegetarian enthusiast or not, to do more pressure cooking at home.

Chapter 1: Pressure Cooking Overview

Pressure Cooking

Pressure-cooking involves boiling a liquid, such as water or broth, in a sealed container to increase the pressure and temperature inside. When the liquid starts boiling, the trapped steam can increase the internal pressure up to 15 pounds per square inch. The increased internal pressure can make the temperature climb up to 250°F. The increased temperature can cook the food faster.

Foods that can be cooked in steam can also be cooked in the pressure cooker. With pressure-cooking, leafy vegetables usually take a minute to cook, legumes take three minutes, and starchy vegetables seven minutes.

Since pressure cooking significantly reduces cooking time, electricity and gas consumption could be lowered by 70 percent. Aside from that, pressure cooking infuses flavors, making foods tastier. It also retains the food's vitamins, minerals and other nutrients, making each meal healthier.

Pressure Cooker Operation

The maximum operating pressure of most pressure cookers is between 11.6 psi to 15 psi. Most stovetop pressure cookers stick to the standard 15 psi. On the other hand, most electric pressure cookers operate in lower pressures. Cooking in electric pressure cookers require additional time to achieve results similar to stovetop pressure cookers.

You should never use your pressure cooker for deep-frying, pan-frying and roasting; however, you can use it to sauté. However, extra care must be taken when cooking foods high in natural sugar such as tomatoes, onions and leeks. They tend to caramelize and stick to the pan of the pressure cooker.

The basic technique in pressure-cooking is to throw in all the ingredients in the pressure cooker, close and lock the lid and then bring the pressure cooker to high pressure. Another technique is to sauté the ingredients first in the pressure cooker before adding the liquid and then bringing it to high pressure. When cooking time is up, the lid can only be opened when the pressure is gone.

Pressure Release Methods

- Cold water release – This is the fastest way to release pressure. It is done by running cold tap water over the lid of the pressure cooker. The pressure can go down in as fast as 20 seconds. This method is only recommended for stovetop pressure cookers.

- Quick release – This is also called normal release. This is done by removing or lifting the valve to release the pressure. Caution must be taken in releasing the steam as the superheated contents of the pot could spray outwards as well. It could take two to three minutes to completely release the pressure using the quick release method. This method is recommended when food cooks easily. Examples of foods that cook easily are leafy vegetables and legumes.

- Natural release – This method allows pressure to go down naturally at room temperature. Stovetop pressure cookers need about 10 to 15 minutes to let the pressure go down, while electric pressure cookers need about 20 to 25 minutes. This method is recommended when food takes longer to cook. Examples of foods that take longer to cook are grains, beans and pasta.

Chapter 2: Pressure Cooked Breakfast Meals

1. Baked Red Apples

Ingredients:

- 6 red apples, cored

- 1 tablespoon dried currants

- ¼ cup dried apricots, chopped

- 1 teaspoon cinnamon

- ¼ teaspoon nutmeg

- 1 cup sweetened apple juice

- ½ cup brown sugar

Procedure:

1. Place the apples in the pressure cooker.

2. In a bowl, combine sweetened apple juice, brown sugar, cinnamon and nutmeg. Pour mixture over the apples. Add the dried apricots and dried currants to the apples.

3. Put the lid of the pressure cooker on and lock it in place. If you are using an

electric pressure cooker, set it to high pressure and cook for 13 minutes. If you are using a stovetop pressure cooker, cook over high heat until high pressure is reached. Lower the heat, maintain pressure and cook for 10 minutes.

4. When the cooking time is up, release the pressure using the natural release method. Transfer the apples to individual bowls. Pour the remaining cooking liquid over the apples and serve immediately.

2. Easy Millet Pilaf

Ingredients:

- 2 cups decorticated millet

- 1 tablespoon coconut oil

- 1 white onion, sliced thinly

- 3 cups water

- 1 bay leaf

- 1 teaspoon cardamom, crushed

- 1 teaspoon cumin seeds

- 1 teaspoon cinnamon

- 1 teaspoon salt

Procedure:

1. Pre-heat the pressure cooker's base and then add oil. Add the cardamom, cumin seeds, bay leaf and cinnamon to the oil. Stir and cook for about 1 minute or until cumin seeds begin to make a crackling sound.

2. Add onion slices to the mixture. Continue to cook for 5 minutes or until they become soft and translucent. Add

millet, water and salt into the pressure cooker. Stir well to combine.

3. Close the pressure cooker's lid and lock it. Bring the pressure cooker to high pressure. This would take 3 minutes to cook in an electric pressure cooker and 2 minutes in a stovetop pressure cooker.

4. When the cooking time is up, let the pressure go down naturally for about 10 minutes. Release the remaining pressure through the pressure cooker's valve.

5. Use a fork to fluff the millet. Put the millet pilaf into a bowl and serve immediately.

3. Simple Lentil Risotto

Ingredients:

- 1 cup dry lentils
- 1 cup long-grain rice
- 2 sprigs parsley, chopped
- 1 white onion, chopped
- 2 tablespoons extra-virgin olive oil
- 1 rib celery, sliced thinly
- 3 cups vegetable stock
- 3 cloves garlic, minced

Procedure:

1. Soak the lentils overnight. Strain them and then set aside.

2. Heat half of the olive oil in the pressure cooker. Add onion and sauté until it becomes soft and translucent. Add the parsley and celery into the pressure cooker and continue to sauté for about 1 minute.

3. Put the rice and garlic into the pressure cooker. Stir and continue to cook for

another 1 minute, stirring constantly. Add the vegetable stock and the lentils into the pressure cooker. Stir well.

4. Put the lid of the pressure cooker on and lock it in place. Set the pressure cooker to high pressure. If an electric pressure cooker is used, cook for 7 minutes. If a stovetop pressure cooker is used, cook for 5 minutes.

5. Release the pressure through the pressure cooker's valve. Mix well and transfer some lentil risotto into a bowl. Drizzle with olive oil and serve immediately.

4. Asparagus Risotto

Ingredients:

- 1 bunch asparagus, about 500 grams

- 2 cups long-grain rice

- 1 red onion, chopped

- 2 tablespoons extra-virgin olive oil

- 4 cups water

- ¼ cup white wine

- 1 teaspoon fresh lemon juice

- 2 teaspoons salt

Procedure:

1. Rinse the asparagus and cut away the asparagus tips and set them aside. Slice the stems into small rondelles and put them in the pressure cooker.

2. Add the water to the asparagus rondelles and stir. Close the lid of the pressure cooker and lock it.

3. If you are using an electric cooker, set it to high pressure and cook for 12 minutes. If you are using a stovetop

pressure cooker, cook over high heat until you achieve maximum pressure. Lower the heat just enough to maintain pressure. Cook for 10 minutes.

4. Release the pressure through the pressure cooker's valve. Transfer the pressure cooker's contents into a large bowl. Separate the stock from the asparagus stem.

5. Heat the olive oil in the pressure cooker. Add onion and cook until soft and translucent.

6. Add the rice to the cooker and stir to combine. Cook for about two minutes or until rice begin to dry. Pour the white wine over the rice and stir. Continue to cook until liquid has evaporated completely.

7. Add the asparagus tips and asparagus stock to the cooker. Season with salt and stir to well.

8. Close the lid and lock it in place. In an electric pressure cooker, this would cook for 8 minutes. In a stovetop pressure cooker, this would cook for 6 minutes.

9. Release the pressure through the pressure cooker's valve. Open the pressure cooker's lid and pour the lemon juice over the risotto. Stir to combine. Place some of the risotto into a bowl and drizzle with olive oil before serving.

5. *Coco Almond Oats*

Ingredients:

- 1 cup coarse oatmeal

- 1 tablespoon coconut oil

- 4 cups coconut milk

- 2 tablespoon maple syrup

- ¼ cup shredded coconut, sweetened

- ¼ cup almonds, slivered

- ¼ teaspoon salt

Procedure:

1. Heat coconut oil in the pressure cooker. Add oats and stir constantly for about 3 minutes or until oats smell nutty and lightly toasted. Add coconut milk and salt to the oats and then mix well.

2. Close the pressure cooker's lid and lock it. For electric pressure cooker, cooking time is 12 minutes. For stovetop pressure cooker, cooking time is 10 minutes after high pressure is achieved.

3. When the cooking time is up, let the pressure go down naturally for 10

minutes. Release the remaining pressure through the pressure cooker's valve.

4. Open the pressure cooker's lid and add maple syrup to the oats. Stir the mixture well until it thickens. Serve in a bowl and top with almonds and shredded coconut before serving.

6. *Berry Breakfast Quinoa*

Ingredients:

- 1 cup uncooked quinoa

- 2 tablespoons maple syrup

- 2 cups water

- ½ teaspoon cinnamon

- 1 teaspoon vanilla

- ½ teaspoon salt

- ½ cup almond milk

- ¼ cup almonds, slivered

- ¼ cup fresh strawberries, halved

- ¼ cup fresh blackberries, halved

Procedure:

1. Rinse quinoa and drain well. Put quinoa, water, cinnamon, vanilla and salt into the pressure and mix well.

2. Close the lid and lock it in place. If you are using an electric pressure cooker, set it to and cook for 2 minutes. If you are using a stovetop pressure cooker, cook

23

over high heat until high pressure is reached. Lower the heat and cook for 1 minute.

3. Let the pressure go down naturally for 10 minutes. Release the remaining pressure through the pressure cooker's valve.

4. Open the pressure cooker's lid and fluff the quinoa using a fork. Place some quinoa into a bowl and add some almond milk. Stir well to combine. Top with almonds, strawberries and blackberries and then serve immediately.

7. *Almond Cherry Risotto*

Ingredients:

- 2 cups short-grain rice

- 4 cups almonds milk

- 2 tablespoons coconut oil

- 1 ½ cup apple juice

- 2 red apples, diced

- 1 cup brown sugar

- 2 teaspoons cinnamon

- 1 teaspoon salt

- ½ cup dried cherries, chopped

Procedure:

1. Heat coconut oil in the pressure cooker. Add rice into the pressure cooker and stir to coat. Toast rice for about 5 minutes or until it is opaque.

2. Add brown sugar, apples, cinnamon and salt to the rice and then mix well. Pour the apple juice and almond milk over the mixture and stir well.

3. Put the lid on the pressure cooker on and lock it in place. Bring the pressure cooker to high pressure. This would take 8 minutes to cook in an electric pressure cooker and 5 minutes in a stovetop pressure cooker.

4. Release the pressure through the pressure cooker's valve using the quick release method. Open the pressure cooker's lid and transfer some risotto into a bowl. Top with dried cherries and then serve immediately.

8. Spiced Oatmeal

Ingredients:

- 1 cup coarse oats

- 1 cups carrots, grated

- 4 cups water

- 1 tablespoons coconut oil

- ½ cup brown sugar

- ½ cup raisins

- 1 teaspoon pumpkin spice

- 2 teaspoons cinnamon

- ½ teaspoon salt

- 2 tablespoons chia seeds

- 2 tablespoons cashew nuts, chopped

Procedure:

1. Heat coconut oil in the pressure cooker. Add oats and stir for four minutes to toast them. Put carrots, cinnamon, brown sugar, pumpkin spice, salt, and water into the pressure cooker and stir well.

2. Close the pressure cooker's lid and lock it. Set the pressure cooker to high pressure. If an electric pressure cooker is used, cook for 10 minutes. If a stovetop pressure cooker is used, cook for 8 minutes.

3. When cooking done, wait for 10 minutes to let the pressure go down naturally. Release the remaining pressure doing a quick pressure release.

4. Open the pressure cooker's lid. Add the chia seeds and the raisins to the oats and then stir well until the mixture thickens. Serve the oats in a bowl and top with cashew nuts and then serve immediately.

9. Brussels Sprouts Risotto

Ingredients:

- 2 cups short-grain rice

- 4 cups vegetable stock

- 1 cup Brussels sprouts, halved

- 1 red bell pepper, seeded and chopped

- 1 teaspoon apple cider vinegar

- 1 teaspoon yellow mustard

- 1 clove garlic, minced

- 2 tablespoons soy sauce

- 1 tablespoon maple syrup

- 1 tablespoon vegetable oil

- ½ teaspoon salt

- ¼ teaspoon pepper

Procedure:

1. Heat vegetable oil in the pressure cooker. Add garlic and bell pepper and then sauté for about 3 minutes. Add rice, vegetable stock, yellow mustard, apple

29

cider vinegar, maple syrup and Brussels sprouts. Stir well.

2. Put the lid of the pressure cooker on and lock it in place. In an electric pressure cooker, this would cook for 8 minutes. In a stovetop pressure cooker, this would cook for 5 minutes.

3. Release the pressure using the quick release method. Add soy sauce, salt and pepper to the risotto and stir to combine. Transfer some risotto into a bowl and then serve immediately.

10. Jackfruit Sandwich

Ingredients:

- 2 cups jackfruit in brine, rinsed and drained

- 1 ½ water

- 1 clove garlic, minced

- 1 onion, chopped finely

- 1 teaspoon yellow mustard

- 2 tablespoons tomato paste

- ½ teaspoon cayenne pepper

- 1 teaspoon red wine vinegar

- 1 tablespoon maple syrup

- ½ teaspoon salt

- ¼ teaspoon pepper

- 1 tablespoon pickle relish

- 2 slices wheat bread

- 1 tablespoon vegetable oil

Procedure:

1. Heat vegetable oil in the pressure cooker. Add onion and sauté until caramelized. Add garlic and sauté until fragrant. Add tomato paste, red wine vinegar, maple syrup, mustard, cayenne pepper, salt and pepper. Add water and stir to combine.

2. Close the lid and lock it in place. Cook for 5 minutes in an electric pressure cooker. If you are using a stovetop pressure cooker, start to time when high pressure is achieved and then cook for 3 minutes.

3. When cooking done, let the pressure go down for 10 minutes. Release the remaining pressure through the pressure cooker's valve.

4. Place jackfruit into a bowl and let it cool. Use a fork to shred the jackfruit. Spread some jackfruit on a slice of bread. Top with pickle and serve.

11. *Chickpea Pilaf*

Ingredients:

- 1 cup white rice

- 2 cups water

- 1 cup chickpeas, rinsed and drained

- 1 teaspoon ginger, grated

- 1 red onion, chopped

- 2 cloves garlic, minced

- ½ teaspoon cumin seeds

- ½ teaspoon cayenne pepper

- ½ teaspoon turmeric

- ¼ teaspoon cinnamon

- ¼ teaspoon coriander

- ¼ teaspoon nutmeg

- 1 cup tomato, diced

- ½ cup cauliflower, chopped

- 2 tablespoons fresh lemon juice

- 2 tablespoons cilantro, chopped

- 1 teaspoon salt

- 1 teaspoon sugar

- 1 tablespoon vegetable oil

Procedure:

1. Heat the vegetable oil in the pressure cooker. Add cumin and cook until lightly toasted. Add onion and sugar and then cook until caramelized. Add garlic, ginger, cayenne, turmeric, cinnamon, coriander and nutmeg. Stir and cook for about 3 minutes.

2. Add tomatoes, cauliflower, chickpeas, rice and water. Season with salt and then stir to combine.

3. Close the pressure cooker's lid and lock it. For electric pressure cooker, cooking time is 10 minutes. For stovetop pressure cooker, cooking time is 8 minutes after high pressure is achieved.

4. Allow the pressure to go down naturally for 10 minutes. Release the remaining pressure through the pressure cooker's valve.

5. Add lemon juice and fluff pilaf using a fork. Put the pilaf into a bowl. Sprinkle with cilantro and then serve immediately.

12. Brown Rice Salad

Ingredients:

- 2 cups brown rice

- 1 cup chickpeas

- 4 cups water

- 1 cup cherry tomatoes, quartered

- ¼ cup fresh cilantro, chopped

- 1 avocado, diced

- 2 cups baby spinach

- 2 teaspoons hot sauce

- 5 tablespoons lime juice

- 5 tablespoons olive oil

- 1 tablespoons honey

- 1 clove garlic, minced

- ¼ cup pine nuts, toasted

- 1/2 teaspoon salt

Procedure:

1. Soak chickpeas overnight. Rinse chickpeas, drain well and then put them

36

in the pressure cooker. Put rice, water and salt into the pressure cooker and stir well.

2. Close the lid and lock it in place. Set electric pressure cooker to high pressure and cook for 12 minutes. If a stovetop pressure cooker is used, bring to high pressure and cook for 10 minutes.

3. After cooking, let the pressure go down naturally for 10 minutes. Release the remaining pressure through the pressure cooker's valve.

4. Use a fork to fluff rice and chickpeas. Transfer them to a large bowl. Add avocado, tomatoes and cilantro to the bowl and then toss to combine.

5. In a separate bowl, whisk limejuice together with garlic, hot sauce, honey, olive oil, and salt. Pour the mixture over the salad and toss gently.

6. Arrange baby spinach on a plate. Place some salad mixture on the bed of spinach and top with pine nuts. Serve immediately.

13. Tempeh Tacos

Ingredients:

- 1 block tempeh, diced
- 1 cup water
- 2 tablespoons vegetable oil
- 1 medium carrot, diced
- 1 large onion, diced
- 1 medium turnip, diced
- ½ cup sauerkraut
- 1 cup cabbage, shredded
- 1 teaspoon salt
- 4 taco shells

Procedure:

1. Heat vegetable oil in a pan. Pan-fry the tempeh until all sides are browned.

2. Put the tempeh in the pressure cooker. Add onion, carrot, turnip, cabbage and sauerkraut. Add water into the pressure cooker. Season with salt but do not stir.

3. Put the lid of the pressure cooker on and lock it in place. If you are using an electric pressure cooker, set it to high pressure and cook for 8 minutes. If you are using a stovetop pressure cooker, cook over high heat until it reaches maximum pressure. Lower the heat, maintain pressure and cook for 5 minutes.

4. Release pressure using the quick release method. Transfer vegetables into a bowl to cool. Scoop some vegetables into taco shells and serve immediately.

14. Garden Macaroni Stew

Ingredients:

- 1 cup macaroni pasta
- 2 cups vegetable stock
- 1 cup fresh corn kernel
- 1 cup carrots, diced
- 1 cup zucchini, diced
- 1 can kidney beans, rinsed and drained
- 1 stalk celery, diced
- 1 red onion, chopped
- 2 cups tomatoes, seeded and chopped
- 3 cloves garlic, minced
- 2 cups baby spinach
- 3 tablespoons fresh basil, chopped
- 1 teaspoon salt
- ½ teaspoon pepper
- 2 tablespoons olive oil

Procedure:

1. Heat olive oil in the pressure cooker. Add onion and sauté for 5 minutes or until onion is softened. Add garlic, carrot, zucchini, celery and corn into the pressure cooker. Stir and cook for 3 minutes more.

2. Add vegetable stock, tomatoes, macaroni pasta and salt into the pressure cooker. Mix well.

3. Close the pressure cooker's lid and lock it. Bring the pressure cooker to high pressure. This would take 8 minutes to cook in an electric pressure cooker and 5 minutes in a stovetop pressure cooker.

4. When cooking time is up, release the pressure using the quick release method. Add basil, kidney beans and spinach. Season the soup with pepper and stir well. Put the stew into individual bowls and serve immediately.

15. *Veggie Quinoa Medley*
Ingredients:

- 1 cup quinoa

- 1 eggplant, cubed

- 1 cups water

- 1 red bell pepper, diced

- 1 yellow pepper, diced

- 1 green bell pepper, diced

- 1 onion, chopped

- 1 clove garlic, minced

- 1 zucchini, cubed

- 1 cup chickpeas, rinsed and drained

- 1 cup tomatoes, diced

- 1 teaspoon dried oregano

- 1 teaspoon salt

- ¼ teaspoon pepper

- 2 tablespoons olive oil

- ½ cup fresh basil, chopped

Procedure:

1. Heat olive oil in the pressure cooker. Add onion and sauté until tender. Add garlic, bell peppers, eggplant, zucchini, and 3 tablespoons water. Stir and cook for 2 minutes. Add tomatoes and cook until it starts to release its juices.

2. Add water, dried oregano, chickpeas and quinoa. Stir to combine. Season it with salt and pepper.

3. Close the lid and lock it in place. Set the pressure cooker to high pressure. If an electric pressure cooker is used, cook for 8 minutes. If a stovetop pressure cooker is used, cook for 5 minutes.

4. Release pressure using quick release method. Fluff the quinoa using a fork. Transfer the quinoa into a bowl. Top with chopped basil and then serve immediately.

16. Spicy Refried Mixed Beans

Ingredients:

- 2 cups mixed beans, rinsed and drained
- 1 teaspoon chili powder
- ½ teaspoon cumin
- ½ teaspoon chipotle powder
- 1 tablespoon olive oil
- 1 white onion, chopped
- 1 bunch cilantro, chopped
- 2 cups vegetable stock
- 1 teaspoon salt
- ½ teaspoon pepper

Procedure:

1. Heat olive oil in the pressure cooker. Cook onion for about 2 minutes or until softened. Add parsley, onion and chipotle powder. Mix and continue to cook for a minute more. Add vegetable stock and beans into the pressure cooker.

2. Put the lid of the pressure cooker on and lock it in place. In an electric pressure cooker, this would cook for 10 minutes. In a stovetop pressure cooker, this would cook for 7 minutes.

3. Wait for 10 minutes to let the pressure go down. Release the remaining pressure through the pressure cooker's valve.

4. Put the beans into a bowl and mash according to the desired consistency. Season the mashed beans with salt and pepper. Garnish with chopped parsley before serving.

17. Eggplant Tofu Marinara

Ingredients:

- 1 250-gram firm tofu, diced
- 1 cup marinara sauce
- ½ cup water
- 3 eggplants, cubed
- 2 tablespoons olive oil
- 1 clove garlic, minced
- 2 tablespoons fresh parsley, chopped
- 1 teaspoon salt
- ¼ pepper

Procedure:

1. Heat olive oil in the pressure cooker. Add tofu and cook until slightly browned. Add garlic and cook until fragrant. Add eggplant and cook for 2 minutes. Add marinara sauce and water. Season it with salt and pepper. Stir to combine.

2. Close the pressure cooker's lid and lock it. Cook for 8 minutes in an electric

pressure cooker. If you are using a stovetop pressure cooker, start to time when high pressure is achieved and then cook for 5 minutes.

3. Release pressure using the quick release method. Transfer the pressure cooker's contents into a bowl. Garnish with chopped parsley and then serve.

Chapter 3: Pressure Cooked Lunch Meals

1. Rice and Bean Stew

Ingredients:

- 1 cup dried mung beans
- ½ cup brown rice
- 1 large onion, chopped
- 2 cloves garlic, chopped
- ½ teaspoon cumin seeds
- 1 teaspoon ginger, grated
- 1 large tomato, chopped
- ½ teaspoon turmeric
- ½ teaspoon cayenne pepper
- 1 teaspoon salt
- ¼ teaspoon pepper
- 4 cups water
- 1 tablespoon vegetable oil

Procedure:

1. Heat vegetable oil in the pressure cooker. Add cumin seeds and cook until fragrant. Add onion and sauté until tender. Add garlic, ginger, turmeric and cayenne pepper. Stir and cook for 2 minutes.

2. Add tomatoes and 3 tablespoons water. Stir and cook until tomatoes have released juice. Add beans, rice and water. Season the mixture with salt and pepper. Stir to combine.

3. Close the pressure cooker's lid and lock it in place. For electric pressure cooker, cooking time is 15 minutes. For stovetop pressure cooker, cooking time is 12 minutes after high pressure is achieved.

4. When cooking is done, allow the pressure to go down naturally for 10 minutes. Release the remaining pressure using the quick release method. Serve in a bowl and serve immediately.

2. Spicy Black Eyed Peas Curry

Ingredients:

- 1 cup black eyed peas
- 1 cup tomatoes, diced
- 1 tablespoon tomato paste
- 1 white onion, chopped
- 2 cloves garlic, chopped
- 1 teaspoon ginger, grated
- 1 teaspoon red chili flakes
- 1 teaspoon brown sugar
- ½ teaspoon cumin
- ½ teaspoon coriander
- ½ teaspoon turmeric
- 2 cups water
- 1 teaspoon salt
- ½ teaspoon pepper
- 1 tablespoon vegetable oil
- 2 tablespoons cilantro, chopped

Procedure:

1. Heat vegetable oil in the pressure cooker. Add onion and sauté until tender. Add garlic, ginger, red chili flakes, turmeric, coriander and cumin. Stir and cook for about 2 minutes.

2. Add tomatoes and tomato paste. Mix well and cook for about 5 minutes or until mixture thickens. Add black eyed peas, sugar, salt and pepper. Stir well.

3. Put the lid of the pressure cooker on and lock it in place. Set electric pressure cooker to high pressure and cook for 12 minutes; for stovetop pressure cookers, bring to maximum pressure and allow to cook for 8 minutes.

4. Let the pressure go down naturally for 10 minutes. Release remaining pressure through the pressure cooker's valve. Put some curry into a bowl, garnish with cilantro and serve immediately.

3. Barley and Lentil Stew

Ingredients:

- 1 cup lentils
- ½ cup pearl barley
- 1 cup tomatoes, diced
- 1 large carrot, diced
- 1 large onion, chopped
- 1 clove garlic, minced
- 4 cups vegetable stock
- 1 tablespoon olive oil
- 1 teaspoon salt
- ¼ teaspoon pepper

Procedure:

1. Heat olive oil in the pressure. Add onion and sauté until tender. Add garlic and tomatoes. Stir and cook for about 2 minutes. Add carrots, lentil and barley. Add water and stir to combine. Season it with salt and pepper.

2. Close the lid and lock it in place. If you are using an electric pressure cooker, set it to high pressure and cook for 15 minutes. If you are using a stovetop pressure cooker, cook over high heat until it reaches maximum pressure. Lower the heat. Make sure to maintain pressure and cook for 10 minutes.

3. Allow the pressure to go down naturally for 10 minutes. Release remaining pressure through the pressure cooker's valve. Transfer stew into a bowl and serve warm.

4. Creamy Polenta

Ingredients:

- 1 cup cornmeal

- 2 cups water

- 2 cups almond milk

- 1 teaspoon salt

- 3 tablespoons maple syrup

Procedure:

1. Heat water and almond milk in the pressure cooker. Gradually add the cornmeal and whisk to prevent lumps from forming. Season it with and stir.

2. Close the pressure cooker's lid and lock it. Bring the pressure cooker to high pressure. This would take 8 minutes to cook in an electric pressure cooker and 5 minutes in a stovetop pressure cooker.

3. After cooking, let the pressure go down naturally for 10 minutes, if there is still a bit of pressure left, open the release valve.

4. Whisk the polenta and serve it into a bowl. Drizzle maple syrup and serve immediately.

5. Mashed Potato with Garlic

Ingredients:

- 3 large Yukon gold potatoes

- 1 cup almond milk

- 1 cup water

- 1 teaspoon salt

- ½ teaspoon pepper

- 1 tablespoon olive oil

- 2 cloves garlic, minced

Procedure:

1. Heat olive oil in a pan. Add garlic and cook until golden. Set it aside.

2. Peel potatoes and cut them into chunks. Place them in the pressure cooker and cove them with water. Add salt and garlic to the potatoes and then stir to combine.

3. Close the lid and lock it in place. Set the pressure cooker to high pressure. If an electric pressure cooker is used, cook for 10 minutes. If a stovetop pressure cooker is used, cook for 8 minutes.

4. Release the pressure using the quick release method. Mash the potatoes. Gradually add almond milk and continue to mash to desired consistency. Season with salt and pepper.

5. Scoop the mashed potato place it on a plate. Drizzle with extra-virgin olive oil and then serve immediately.

6. Penne with Mushroom

Ingredients:

- 1 250-gram pack penne

- 1 cup button mushrooms, chopped

- 2 cups water

- 2 onions, chopped

- 2 cloves garlic, minced

- 1 teaspoon fennel seeds

- 4 cups tomato puree

- ½ teaspoon red pepper flakes

- 1 teaspoon salt

- ¼ cup parsley, chopped

- 1 tablespoon olive oil

Procedure:

1. Heat olive oil in the pressure cooker. Add onion and fennel deeds and then sauté until tender. Add mushrooms and cook until slightly browned. Add garlic and cook until fragrant.

2. Add water and salt and then stir well. Scrape the bottom of the pressure cooker. Add pasta and tomato puree.

3. Put the lid of the pressure cooker on and lock it in place. In an electric pressure cooker, this would cook for 8 minutes. In a stovetop pressure cooker, this would cook for 5 minutes.

4. Release the pressure using the quick release method. Stir to combine and then transfer pasta into a bowl. Top with chopped parsley and then serve.

7. *Tomato Pasta*

Ingredients:

- 1 250-gram pasta shells

- 1 cup vegetable stock

- 2 cups water

- 1 cup sun-dried tomatoes

- 1 cup raw cashew nuts

- 1 teaspoon red pepper flakes

- 1 tablespoon fresh lemon juice

- 1 onion, chopped

- 2 cloves garlic, chopped

- 1 teaspoon salt

- ¼ teaspoon pepper

- 1 tablespoon olive oil

- ¼ cup basil leaves, chopped

Procedure:

1. Place vegetable stock, tomatoes, cashew nuts, garlic and lemon juice in a blender. Blend until smooth.

2. Heat olive oil in the pressure cooker. Add onion and sauté until tender. Add pasta, water and tomato mixture into the pressure cooker. Stir well.

3. Close the lid and lock it in place. Cook for 12 minutes in an electric pressure cooker. If you are using a stovetop pressure cooker, start the timer upon achieving maximum pressure and then cook for 10 minutes.

4. Let the pressure go down naturally for 10 minutes. Release remaining pressure through the pressure cooker's valve. Stir pasta. Transfer pasta into a bowl. Top with chopped basil and then serve.

8. Sweet Spicy Penne Pasta

Ingredients:

- 1 25-gram penne
- 2 cups water
- 1 cup tomato puree
- 1 onion, sliced thinly
- 3 tablespoons olive oil
- 3 cloves garlic, minced
- 1 teaspoon dried oregano
- 1 teaspoon red chili flakes
- 2 tablespoons sugar
- ½ teaspoon salt
- ¼ teaspoon pepper
- ¼ cup fresh parsley, chopped

Procedure:

1. Heat olive oil in the pressure cooker. Add onion and sauté until tender. Add red chili flakes, basil, oregano, and garlic. Sauté until fragrant.

2. Add water and pasta into the pressure cooker. Scrape the bottom of the pressure cooker. Add tomato puree, salt and sugar. Mix well.

3. Close the pressure cooker's lid and lock it. For electric pressure cooker, cooking time is 10 minutes. For stovetop pressure cooker, cooking time is 8 minutes after achieving maximum pressure.

4. When cooking time is up, let the pressure go down naturally for 10 minutes. Release the remaining pressure through the pressure cooker's valve. Stir pasta and transfer it into a bowl. Top with chopped basil and then serve.

9. *Black Beans Chili*

Ingredients:

- 2 cups dried black beans

- 3 cups water

- 2 cloves garlic, minced

- 1 red bell pepper, seeded and chopped

- 1 green bell pepper, seeded and chopped

- 1 red onion, chopped

- 1 tablespoon ground cumin

- 1 tablespoon chili powder

- 1 tablespoon tomato paste

- 1 cup tomatoes, chopped

- 1 tablespoon chipotle, minced

- 2 tablespoons vegetable oil

- 1 cup corn kernel

Procedure:

1. Soak the beans overnight. Rinse the beans and drain well.

2. Heat the vegetable oil in the pressure cooker. Add onion, garlic and bell peppers. Sauté until onion is tender and garlic is fragrant.

3. Add cumin and chili power. Stir and cook for about 1 minute. Add chipotles and tomato paste. Stir and cook for another minute. Add tomatoes, beans and water. Season with salt and then stir well.

4. Put the lid of the pressure cooker on and lock it in place. Set electric pressure cooker to high pressure and cook for 15 minutes. If a stovetop pressure cooker is used, bring to high pressure and cook for 12 minutes.

5. Allow the pressure go down naturally for 10 minutes. Release remaining pressure through the pressure cooker's valve. Put the beans into a bowl and serve warm.

10. Zesty Tempeh

Ingredients:

- 1 25-gram tempeh, cubed
- 1 medium sweet potato, cubed
- 1 medium carrot, cubed
- 1 cup vegetable stock
- 1 onion, chopped
- 1 clove garlic, chopped
- 3 tablespoon fresh lemon juice
- 1 teaspoon lemon zest
- 2 tablespoon fresh parsley, chopped
- 1 tablespoon olive oil
- 1 teaspoon salt

Procedure:

1. Heat olive oil in the pressure cooker. Add onion and sauté until tender. Add garlic and sauté until fragrant. Add tempeh and cook until slightly browned. Add carrot, sweet potato, vegetable stock and salt. Stir to combine.

66

2. Close the lid and lock it in place. If you are using an electric pressure cooker, set it to high pressure and cook for 5 minutes. If you are using a stovetop pressure cooker, cook over high heat until high pressure is reached. Lower the heat but maintain pressure. Cook for 3 minutes.

3. Release pressure using quick release method. Put the vegetables into a bowl. Pour some lemon juice on the vegetables. Top with lemon zest and then serve.

11. Tofu Curry

Ingredients:

- 1 250-gram pack firm tofu, cubed

- 2 cups water

- 1 large potato, cubed

- 1 large carrot, cut into 1 inch rondelles

- 1 cup cabbage, shredded

- 1 cup edamame

- 1 red onion, chopped

- 1 teaspoon ginger, grated

- 1 red bell pepper, chopped

- 3 cloves garlic, minced

- 1 teaspoon cumin seeds

- 1 teaspoon coriander

- 2 teaspoons curry paste

- 3 tablespoons tomato paste

- 3 tablespoons coconut oil

- 1 teaspoon salt

- ½ teaspoon pepper

Procedure:

1. Heat coconut oil in the pressure cooker. Add cumin seeds and stir until they crackle. Add onion and sauté until translucent. Add coriander, ginger, bell pepper, curry paste and salt. Mix well and sauté for 1 minute.

2. Add tomato paste and three tablespoons water. Stir well to combine. Add tofu, carrots, potatoes and cabbage into the pressure cooker. Add water to the mixture and stir.

3. Close the lid of the pressure cooker and lock it in place. Bring the pressure cooker to high pressure. This would take 5 minutes to cook in an electric pressure cooker and 3 minutes in a stovetop pressure cooker.

4. Release pressure using the quick release pressure method. Transfer curry into a bowl and serve warm with steamed rice.

12. Spiced Chickpea Stew
Ingredients:

- 1 cup chickpeas

- 1 cup rice

- 3 ½ cups water

- 1 tablespoon vegetable oil

- 2 cloves garlic, minced

- 1 red onion, sliced thinly

- 1 teaspoon ginger, grated

- 2 tablespoon tomato paste

- 1 teaspoon salt

- ¼ teaspoon coriander

- ¼ teaspoon cumin

- ¼ teaspoon nutmeg

- ¼ teaspoon cardamom

- ¼ teaspoon chili powder

Procedure:

1. Soak chickpeas overnight. Rinse chickpeas and drain well. Set them aside.

2. Place rice in 4-cup heat proof dish. Add water 1 ½ cup water to rice, stir it well and then set it aside.

3. Heat vegetable oil in the pressure cooker and sauté onion for 5 minutes. Add ginger, coriander, cumin, nutmeg, cardamom and chili powder. Stir and cook for 1 minute.

4. Add the remaining water, tomato paste and chickpeas into the pressure cooker. Place the dish with rice into the steamer basket and then then lower it into the pressure cooker.

5. Close the pressure cooker's lid and lock it. Set the pressure cooker to high pressure. If an electric pressure cooker is used, cook for 15 minutes. If a stovetop pressure cooker is used, cook for 12 minutes.

6. When cooking is done, let the pressure go down naturally for 10 minutes.

Release the remaining pressure through the pressure cooker's valve.

7. Lift out the steamer from the pressure cooker. Remove the dish and fluff the rice using a fork. Put the chickpeas into a bowl. Serve chickpeas with rice.

13. Creamy Mung Beans

Ingredients:

- 1 cup dry mung beans

- ½ cup tofu, diced

- ½ cup water

- 1 cup cream

- 1 onion, chopped

- 2 cloves garlic, minced

- 1 cup tomatoes, diced

- 1 tablespoons coconut oil

- 2 cups bok choy, chopped

- 1 teaspoon salt

- ½ teaspoon pepper

Procedure:

1. Soak dried mung beans overnight. Rinse the beans, drain well, and set them aside.

2. Heat coconut oil in the pressure cooker. Add tofu and cook until golden. Add onion and sauté until tender. Add garlic

and tomatoes. Stir and cook for 3 minutes.

3. Add water and scrape the bottom of the pan. Make sure nothing sticks there. Add mung beans, bok choy, salt and pepper. Stir to combine.

4. Put the lid of the pressure cooker on and lock it in place. In an electric pressure cooker, this would cook for 5 minutes. In a stovetop pressure cooker, this would cook for 3 minutes.

5. After cooking, let the pressure go down naturally for 10 minutes. Release the remaining pressure through the pressure cooker's valve.

6. Add coconut cream to the mung beans and stir well. Serve while still warm.

14. Sweet Spicy Bean Stew

Ingredients:

- 1 cup kidney beans
- 1 cup black-eyed beans
- 1 cup sweet potatoes, diced
- 1 cup tomatoes, chopped
- 1 tablespoon olive oil
- 1 jalapeno pepper, chopped
- 1 red pepper, chopped
- 1 red onion, chopped
- 1 tablespoon ground coriander
- 1 tablespoon ground cumin
- 1 teaspoon chili flakes
- 2 tablespoons white vinegar
- 4 cups vegetable stock
- 2 teaspoon salt

Procedure:

1. Soak the beans overnight. Rinse the beans and drain well.

75

2. Heat olive oil in the pressure cooker. Sauté onion until becomes translucent. Add jalapeno pepper, chili flakes, red pepper, coriander, cumin and sweet potatoes into the pressure cooker, and continue to cook for about 5 minutes.

3. Add the kidney beans, black-eyed beans, tomatoes, white vinegar and vegetable stock into the pressure cooker.

4. Close the lid and lock it in place. Cook for 13 minutes in an electric pressure cooker. If you are using a stovetop pressure cooker, start to time when high pressure is achieved and then cook for 10 minutes.

5. Wait for about 20 minutes or until the pressure goes down naturally before opening the pressure cooker's lid.

6. Season the beans with salt and stir well. Transfer some beans into a bowl and drizzle olive oil before serving.

15. Sweet Brussels Sprout and Green Beans

Ingredients:

- 2 cups Brussels sprouts, halved

- 1 cup green beans cut into 1 inch length

- 1 large onion, chopped

- 1 tablespoon olive oil

- ½ cup vegetable stock

- 1 tablespoon honey

- 1 tablespoon Dijon mustard

- 1 teaspoon salt

- ½ teaspoon pepper

Procedure:

1. In a small bowl, whisk honey together with the vegetable stock. Set the mixture aside.

2. Heat olive oil in the pressure cooker. Add onion and sauté until tender. Add Brussels sprouts, greens beans and Dijon mustard into the pressure cooker,

and then mix well. Pour the honey mixture over the vegetables.

3. Put the lid of the pressure cooker on and lock it in place. For electric pressure cooker, cooking time is 5 minutes. For stovetop pressure cooker, cooking time is 3 minutes after high pressure is achieved.

4. Release the pressure using the quick release method. Transfer the vegetables into a bowl. Drizzle with olive oil before serving.

16. Veggie with Olives

Ingredients:

- 1 large potato, cubed

- 1 zucchini, cubed

- 1 eggplant, cubed

- 1 onion, chopped

- 8 grape tomatoes, halved

- 1 red bell pepper, diced

- ¼ cup raisins

- ¼ Kalamata olives, pitted

- ¼ cup olive oil

- 1 tablespoon capers, rinsed

- 2 tablespoons pine nuts

- 2 tablespoons basil, chopped

- 1 teaspoon salt

- ¼ teaspoon pepper

Procedure:

1. Heat olive oil in the pressure cooker. Add onion and cook until tender. Add

potatoes and eggplant and then cook for about 2 minutes. Add zucchini and bell pepper and then cook for another 2 minutes.

2. Add raisins, basil, capers, olives, salt, pepper and half of pine nuts. Stir to combine.

3. Close and lock the pressure cooker's lid. Set electric pressure cooker to high pressure and cook for 6 minutes. If a stovetop pressure cooker is used, bring to high pressure and cook for 4 minutes.

4. Release pressure using the quick release method. Add grape tomatoes and stir to combine. Put the vegetables into a bowl. Top with pine nuts and then serve.

17. Eggplant Curry

Ingredients:

- 1 large eggplant, cubed
- 1 large potato, cubed
- 1 large onion, chopped
- ½ cup tomatoes, diced
- 1 green chili, sliced
- ½ teaspoon cumin seeds
- ½ teaspoon turmeric
- ½ teaspoon chili powder
- 2 tablespoons cilantro, chopped
- 2 tablespoons olive oil
- ½ cup vegetable stock
- 1 teaspoon salt
- ¼ teaspoon pepper

Procedure:

1. Heat olive oil in the pressure cooker. Add cumin seeds and cook until they

crackle. Add green chili and onion and then sauté until tender.

2. Add potato and cook for 2 minutes. Add eggplant and cook for 2 minutes. Add tomato and cilantro. Add chili powder, turmeric, salt and pepper. Stir to combine. Add vegetable stock and mix well.

3. Close the pressure cooker's lid and lock it. If you are using an electric pressure cooker, set it to high pressure and cook for 6 minutes. If you are using a stovetop pressure cooker, cook over high heat until high pressure is reached. Lower the heat and cook for 5 minutes.

4. When cooking time is up, let the pressure go down normally for 10 minutes. Release remaining pressure through the pressure cooker's valve. Stir the vegetables. Transfer the curry into a bowl. Serve warm with steamed rice.

Chapter 4: Pressure Cooked Dinner Meals

1. *Mashed Potato*

Ingredients:

- 1 kilo gold potatoes

- 1 cup water

- 2 cups cauliflower florets

- 1 tablespoon nutritional yeast

- 1 teaspoon salt

- ½ teaspoon pepper

Procedure:

1. Peel potatoes and dice them. Place potatoes, cauliflower and water into the pressure cooker.

2. Close and lock the pressure cooker's lid. Bring the pressure cooker to high pressure. This would take 10 minutes to cook in an electric pressure cooker and 8 minutes in a stovetop pressure cooker.

3. When cooking is done, release the pressure using the quick release method. Mash potatoes and cauliflower. Pour olive oil, salt, pepper and nutritional yeast into the pressure cooker and continue to mash to the desired consistency. Scoop the mashed potato and place it on a plate and serve immediately.

2. *Mushroom Risotto*

Ingredients:

- 1 cup short-grain rice

- 1 cup water

- ½ cup mushrooms, chopped

- 2 cups vegetable stock

- 1 white onion, chopped

- 1 teaspoon salt

- ½ teaspoon pepper

Procedure:

1. Heat the olive in the pressure cooker. Add onion and sauté for 3 minutes or until tender. Add rice and stir to coat with oil. Stir constantly and cook for another 3 minutes. Add vegetable stock and water. Stir to combine. Season it with salt and pepper.

2. Close the lid and lock it in place. Set the pressure cooker to high pressure. If an electric pressure cooker is used, cook for 10 minutes. If a stovetop pressure cooker is used, cook for 8 minutes.

3. When cooking time is up, let the pressure go down naturally for 10 minutes. Release the remaining pressure through the pressure cooker's valve.

4. Fluff the risotto using a fork. Transfer the risotto into a bowl. Drizzle olive oil and then serve warm.

3. *Spaghetti with Cauliflower*

Ingredients:

- 1 250-gram pack spaghetti

- 1 head cauliflower, florets separated

- 2 8 oz. cans tomato sauce

- 1 cup water

- 2 cups red wine

- 1 onion, chopped

- 2 cloves garlic, minced

- 1 teaspoon red pepper flakes

- 1 tablespoon olive oil

- ¼ cup parsley, chopped

- 1 teaspoon salt

- ¼ teaspoon pepper

Procedure:

1. Heat olive oil in the pressure cooker. Add onion and sauté until translucent. Add garlic and sauté until fragrant. Add cauliflower, stir and cook for about 2 minutes.

2. Add water, red wine, red pepper flakes, salt and pepper. Break spaghetti in half and then add into the pressure cooker. Stir to combine.

3. Put the lid of the pressure cooker on and lock it in place. In an electric pressure cooker, this would cook for 8 minutes. In a stovetop pressure cooker, this would cook for 5 minutes.

4. Release pressure using quick release method. Stir pasta. Transfer the pasta into a bowl. Top with chopped parsley and then serve.

4. Pumpkin Risotto

Ingredients:

- 4 cups pumpkin, diced

- 2 cups long-grain rice

- 2 tablespoons extra-virgin olive oil

- 1 cups vegetable stock

- ¼ cup white wine

- 3 cloves garlic, chopped

- 2 sprigs sage

- 1 teaspoon nutmeg

- 2 teaspoons salt

Procedure:

1. Heat half of the olive oil in the pressure cooker. Remove the sage leaves from the sprigs, add them to the oil and cook until crispy. Then set the crispy sage leaves aside.

2. Add the remaining olive oil into the pressure cooker. Add garlic to the oil and cook until golden and toasted. Remove the garlic from the cooker and

set aside. Add half of the pumpkin and half of the cooked sage to the cooker. Toss to combine.

3. Cook the pumpkin for about 5 minutes or until browned and caramelized. Remove the pumpkin from the pan and set aside. Add the rice to the cooker and toast it for two to three minutes. Pour the white wine over the rice and continue to toast until liquid has completely evaporated.

4. Add the remaining pumpkin, toasted garlic, vegetable stock and salt to the cooker. Stir well to combine.

5. Close the pressure cooker's lid and lock it. If you are using an electric pressure cooker, set it to high pressure and cook for 8 minutes. If you are using a stovetop pressure cooker, cook over high heat until it attains high pressure. Lower the heat, maintain pressure and cook for 6 minutes.

6. After cooking, release the pressure through the pressure cooker's valve. Put some risotto into a bowl and dust it with nutmeg before serving.

5. Pesto Spaghetti

Ingredients:

- 1 pack spaghetti pasta

- 4 large zucchinis, chopped

- 1 white onion, chopped

- 3 cups fresh basil, firmly packed

- ½ cup water

- 2 tablespoons olive oil

- 3 cloves garlic, minced

- 1 teaspoon salt

Procedure:

1. Cook pasta according to package instructions.

2. Heat half of the olive oil in the pressure cooker. Sauté onion for about 5 minutes until it becomes soft and translucent. Put water, salt and zucchini into the pressure cooker and stir well.

3. Close the lid and lock it in place. Cook for 5 minutes in an electric pressure cooker. If you are using a stovetop

91

pressure cooker, start to time when high pressure is achieved and then cook for 3 minutes.

4. Release the pressure using the quick release method. Transfer the contents into a bowl and let them cool. Put the zucchinis in the blender. Add the garlic and the basil to the blender. Run the blender until the contents are pureed well.

5. Pour the mixture over the pasta and toss to combine. Drizzle with remaining olive oil and then serve.

6. Roasted Potatoes

Ingredients:

- 500 grams baby potatoes

- 4 tablespoons olive oil

- 2 cloves garlic, crushed

- 1 sprig rosemary

- ½ cup vegetable stock

- ½ teaspoon salt

- ¼ teaspoon pepper

Procedure:

1. Heat olive oil in the pressure cooker. Add garlic, baby potatoes and rosemary into the pressure cooker and stir. Cook the potatoes for about 8 minutes or until all sides of potatoes are browned. Pierce each potato with a knife. Add the vegetable stock into the pressure cooker.

2. Close the lid and lock it in place. For electric pressure cooker, cooking time is 7 minutes. For stovetop pressure cooker, cooking time is 5 minutes after high pressure is achieved.

3. Let the pressure go down naturally for 10 minutes. Release the remaining pressure through the pressure cooker's valve. Season the potatoes with salt and pepper. Serve warm.

7. Spinach Penne Pasta

Ingredients:

- 1 pack 500 gram penne

- 3 cups baby spinach

- 2 cloves garlic, minced

- 2 cloves garlic, crushed

- ¼ cup cashew nuts, chopped

- 1 teaspoon salt

- 5 tablespoons olive oil

Procedure:

1. Heat olive oil in the pressure cooker. Add the crushed garlic and spinach into the pressure cooker. Stir and cook for about 8 minutes or until spinach is wilted.

2. Add the penne pasta into the pressure cooker. Cover the pasta with enough water. Season it with salt and stir well.

3. Put the lid of the pressure cooker on and lock it in place. Cook for 10 minutes in an electric pressure cooker. If you are using a stovetop pressure cooker, start

to time when high pressure is achieved and then cook for 8 minutes.

4. Release the pressure through the pressure cooker's valve. Add the minced garlic to the pasta and stir to combine. Transfer pasta into a bowl and top with cashew. Drizzle with olive oil before serving.

8. Lentil Stew

Ingredients:

- 2 cups dry lentils

- 1 cup tomatoes, chopped

- 3 cups water

- 1 red onion, chopped

- 1 red bell pepper, chopped

- 1 stalk celery, chopped finely

- 1 teaspoon salt

- ½ teaspoon pepper

Procedure:

1. Heat the olive oil in the pressure cooker and sauté onion until softened. Add bell pepper and celery into the pressure cooker and continue to sauté for 2 minutes.

2. Add the tomatoes and stir to combine. Season the mixture with salt and pepper. Add the lentils and water into the pressure cooker.

3. Close the lid of the pressure cooker and lock it in place. If you are using an electric pressure cooker, set it to high pressure and cook for 15 minutes. If you are using a stovetop pressure cooker, cook over high heat until high pressure is reached. Adjust heat to maintain pressure and cook for 10 minutes.

4. Let the pressure go down for 10 minutes. Release the remaining pressure through the pressure cooker's valve. Transfer the lentils into a bowl and serve immediately.

9. *Lentil con Chili*

Ingredients:

- 2 cups red lentils
- 3 cups water
- 1 cup tomatoes, diced
- ½ cup tomato paste
- 1 large onion, chopped
- 2 red bell pepper, chopped
- ¼ cup dates, pitted and chopped
- 3 cloves garlic, minced
- 1 tablespoon oregano
- 1 tablespoon parsley flakes
- 1 tablespoon chili powder
- ½ teaspoon red pepper flakes
- 1 teaspoon chipotle powder
- 1 teaspoon paprika
- 2 tablespoons red wine vinegar

Procedure:

1. Place garlic, tomatoes, red bell pepper, dates and a cup of water in a blender. Blend until mixture is smooth and then set aside.

2. Rinse lentils and drain well. Place lentils in the pressure together with the tomato paste, onion, red wine vinegar, oregano, parsley flakes, red pepper flakes, chili powder, chipotle powder and paprika. Add the blended tomatoes into the pressure cooker and stir to combine.

3. Close the pressure cooker's lid and lock it. Bring the pressure cooker to high pressure. This would take 15 minutes to cook in an electric pressure cooker and 10 minutes in a stovetop pressure cooker.

4. When cooking time is up, wait for 10 minutes to let pressure go down naturally. Release remaining pressure through the pressure cooker's valve. Place the chili into a bowl and serve warm.

10. Quinoa Salad

Ingredients:

- 1 cup quinoa

- 2 cups water

- 1 cup edamame

- 1 medium cucumber, chopped

- 1 cup red cabbage, shredded

- 1 medium carrot, shredded

- 1 red onion, sliced thinly

- ½ cup fresh lime juice

- 1 tablespoon tamari

- 2 tablespoons honey

- 1 tablespoon coconut oil

- 1 tablespoon sesame oil

- 1 tablespoon ginger, grated

- ½ teaspoon red pepper flakes

- ¼ cup fresh cilantro, chopped

- ¼ cup fresh basil, chopped

- ½ cup peanuts, chopped

Procedure:

1. Rinse quinoa and drain well. Put quinoa into the pressure cooker. Add water and salt and then mix well.

2. Close the pressure cooker's lid and lock it in place. Set the pressure cooker to high pressure. If an electric pressure cooker is used, cook for 3 minutes. If a stovetop pressure cooker is used, cook for 2 minutes.

3. Let the pressure go down naturally for 10 minutes. Release the remaining pressure through the pressure cooker's valve. Transfer quinoa to a large bowl. Add cucumber, carrots, cabbage, onion and edamame to the bowl and then toss to combine.

4. In a separate bowl, whisk lime juice together with tamari, honey, vegetable oil, sesame oil, grated ginger and red pepper flakes. Pour the mixture over the salad and toss gently. Top with basil, cilantro and chopped peanuts. Serve immediately.

11. Tofu Vegetable Stew

Ingredients:

- 1 250-gram tofu, diced
- 2 cloves garlic, chopped
- 1 onion, chopped
- 1 stalk celery, chopped
- 1 large carrot, chopped
- 1 large zucchini, chopped
- 2 tablespoons tomato paste
- 1 cup tomatoes, diced
- 1 tablespoon cornstarch
- 2 cups vegetable stock
- ½ cup red wine
- 1 tablespoon vegetable oil
- ¼ cup fresh basil, chopped

Procedure:

1. Heat the vegetable oil in the pressure cooker. Add onion and sauté until tender. Add garlic and sauté until

fragrant. Add tofu and cook until slightly browned. Add zucchini, carrot and celery. Stir constantly and cook for about 2 minutes.

2. In a small bowl, mix cornstarch and red wine. Pour the mixture over the vegetables and stir to combine. Stir constantly and cook for about 1 minute. Add vegetable stock, tomato and tomato paste to the vegetables. Stir well and scrape the bottom of the pressure of the cooker.

3. Put the lid of the pressure cooker on and lock it in place. If you are using an electric pressure cooker, set it to high pressure and cook for 10 minutes. If you are using a stovetop pressure cooker, cook over high heat until high pressure is reached. Adjust heat and maintain pressure. Continue to cook for 8 minutes.

4. Release pressure using quick release method. Transfer stew into a bowl and garnish with basil. It can be served with rice or mashed potato.

12. *Coco Tofu Curry*
Ingredients:

- 1 250-gram firm tofu, cubed

- 2 cups water

- 1 medium potato, chopped

- 1 medium sweet potato, chopped

- 1 medium carrot, chopped

- 1 zucchini, chopped

- 1 cup peas

- 1 can chickpeas, rinsed and drained

- 1 can tomatoes, chopped

- 1 leek, sliced thinly

- ½ cup coconut cream

- 1 tablespoon coconut oil

- ¼ cashews, raw

- 1 tablespoon cumin

- 1 tablespoon curry paste

- 1 tablespoon turmeric

Procedure:

1. Put cashews in a pan. Cover them with water and bring to a boil. Reduce heat and simmer for about 3 minutes. Drain cashews and put them in a blender. Add coconut milk to the blender and blend until smooth, and then set it aside.

2. Heat coconut oil in the pressure cooker and sauté leek for 1 minute. Add sweet potatoes, carrots, potatoes, peas and zucchini. Stir and cook vegetables for 2 minutes. Add chickpeas, tomatoes, tofu, cumin, turmeric and curry paste. Stir well.

3. Close the lid and lock it in place. Cook for 15 minutes in an electric pressure cooker. If you are using a stovetop pressure cooker, start to time when high pressure is achieved and then cook for 12 minutes.

4. Release pressure using the quick release pressure method. Pour the coconut cream mixture over the vegetables and stir to combine. Put some curry into a bowl and serve warm with steamed rice.

13. *Veggie Medley*

Ingredients:

- 1 cup broccoli florets
- 1 cup Brussels sprouts, halved
- 1 cup cauliflower florets
- 1 medium potato, cubed
- 1 medium carrot, cubed
- 1 cup tofu, cubed
- 1 clove garlic, minced
- 1 red onion, chopped
- 1 teaspoon ginger, grated
- 1 tablespoon soy sauce
- 1 tablespoon vegetable oil
- ½ teaspoon salt
- ½ teaspoon pepper
- ¼ cup water

Procedure:

1. Heat vegetable oil in the pressure cooker. Add onion into the pressure

107

cooker and sauté until translucent. Add carrots, potatoes, ginger and tofu and then sauté for 2 minutes. Add water, soy sauce, salt and pepper and then stir to combine.

2. Close and lock the pressure cooker's lid. Cook at high pressure for 2 minutes and then release pressure using quick release method. Open the pressure cooker's lid and stir in the broccoli, cauliflower and Brussels sprouts.

3. Close the pressure cooker's lid and lock it. Set the pressure cooker to high pressure. If an electric pressure cooker is used, cook for 3 minutes. If a stovetop pressure cooker is used, cook for 2 minutes.

4. Release pressure through the pressure cooker's valve. Transfer vegetables into a bowl and serve warm.

14. Red Kidney Beans Curry

Ingredients:

- 1 cup red kidney beans
- 4 tomatoes, chopped
- 2 cups water
- 2 tablespoons vegetable oil
- 1 onion, chopped
- 12 cloves garlic, minced
- 1 green chili, chopped
- 1 teaspoon ginger, grated
- ½ teaspoon turmeric
- ½ teaspoon chili powder
- 1 teaspoon cumin seeds
- 1 teaspoon salt

Procedure:

1. Soak red kidney beans overnight. Rinse red kidney beans, drain well and then put then them into the pressure cooker.

2. Add tomatoes, onion, garlic, chili and ginger into the pressure cooker. Add chili powder, cumin seeds, turmeric and salt. Add water and vegetable oil and then stir to combine all ingredients.

3. Put the lid of the pressure cooker on and lock it in place. If you are using an electric pressure cooker, set it to high pressure and cook for 15 minutes. If you are using a stovetop pressure cooker, cook over high heat until high pressure is reached. Maintain the pressure and cook for 12 minutes.

4. When cooking time is up, let the pressure go down naturally for 20 minutes. Release remaining pressure through the pressure cooker's valve. Stir the beans well. Serve warm with steamed rice or wheat bread.

15. *Tangy Pasta*

Ingredients:

- 1 250-gram ziti pasta

- 4 cups vegetable stock

- 1 medium carrot, diced

- 1 cup cherry tomatoes, halved

- 2 cups garbanzo beans, cooked

- 1 red bell pepper, chopped

- 1 green bell pepper, chopped

- 1 yellow bell pepper, chopped

- 2 cloves garlic, chopped

- 1 large red onion, chopped

- 1 lemon, wedge

- 3 tablespoons olive oil

- 2 tablespoons basil, chopped

- 1 teaspoon salt

- ½ teaspoon pepper

Procedure:

1. Heat olive oil in the pressure cooker. Add onion and sauté until tender. Add garlic, red pepper flakes and then sauté until fragrant

2. Add vegetable stock, pasta, carrot, bell peppers, tomatoes, garbanzo beans and lemon. Season it with salt and pepper. Stir to combine.

3. Put the lid of the pressure cooker on and lock it in place. Cook for 12 minutes in an electric pressure cooker. If you are using a stovetop pressure cooker, start to time when high pressure is achieved and then cook for 10 minutes.

4. When cooking time is up, let the pressure go down naturally for 10 minutes. Release the remaining pressure through the pressure cooker's valve. Stir the pasta. Transfer it into a bowl and garnish with chopped basil. Drizzle with olive oil and serve immediately.

16. Mushroom and Tempeh

Ingredients:

- 1 block tempeh, cubed

- 1 tablespoon sesame oil

- 1 cup button mushrooms, sliced thinly

- 1 tablespoon tamari

- 1 red onion, chopped

- 1 red bell pepper, chopped

- 1 green bell pepper, chopped

- ½ cup vegetable stock

- 2 teaspoons sesame seeds, toasted

Procedure:

1. Heat the sesame oil in the pressure cooker. Add onion and sauté until tender. Add mushroom and tempeh and cook for 3 minutes. Add tamari, vegetable stock and salt. Stir to combine.

2. Close the lid and lock it in place. If you are using an electric pressure cooker, set it to high pressure and cook for 8 minutes. If you are using a stovetop

pressure cooker, cook over high heat until high pressure is reached. Lower the heat, maintain pressure and cook for 5 minutes.

3. Release pressure using the quick release method. Put vegetables into a bowl and serve immediately with steamed rice.

17. Bean and Pasta Soup

Ingredients:

- 1 250-gram pack macaroni or ditalini pasta

- 1 cup cannellini beans

- 6 cups water

- 2 cups tomatoes, diced

- 1 onion, chopped

- 2 cloves garlic, chopped

- 1 large carrot, diced

- 1 rib celery, diced

- 1 tablespoon white vinegar

- 3 teaspoons salt

- 1 teaspoon pepper

- ½ teaspoon red pepper flakes

- 1 tablespoon olive oil

- ¼ cup parsley, chopped

Procedure:

1. Soak cannellini beans overnight. Rinse beans and drain well.

2. Heat olive oil in the pressure cooker. Add onion and sauté until tender. Add garlic, red pepper flakes, celery and carrots. Stir and cook for 3 minutes. Add beans, water, tomatoes, salt and pepper into the pressure cooker. Mix well.

3. Close the pressure cooker's lid and lock it. Set electric pressure cooker to high pressure and cook for 15 minutes. If a stovetop pressure cooker is used, bring to high pressure and cook for 12 minutes.

4. When cooking is done, let the pressure go down naturally for 10 minutes. Release the remaining pressure through the pressure cooker's valve. Add white vinegar and stir. Top with chopped parsley and then serve.

Conclusion

I hope that that this book was able to help understand how pressure cooking works and how it can help you cook delicious vegan meals fast.

I also hope that this book was able to help you find inspiration on how to make not just quick and easy to prepare meals but also healthy and tasty vegan foods.

The next step is for you to make sure that you will use all the helpful information that you have gained from this book in all your future meal preparations.

Made in the USA
Lexington, KY
26 June 2017